The Empty Bowl

the empty bowl

Poems of the Holocaust and After

Judith H. Sherman
Foreword by Arthur Kleinman
Afterword by Ilana Gelb

UNIVERSITY OF NEW MEXICO PRESS | ALBUQUERQUE

© 2022 by Judith H. Sherman
Foreword by Arthur Kleinman © 2022 by the University of New Mexico Press
Afterword by Ilana Gelb © 2022 by the University of New Mexico Press
All rights reserved. Published 2022
Printed in the United States of America

ISBN 978-0-8263-6405-0 (paper)
ISBN 978-0-8263-6406-7 (electronic)

Library of Congress Control Number: 2022933142

Founded in 1889, the University of New Mexico sits on the traditional
  homelands of the Pueblo of Sandia. The original peoples of New Mexico—
  Pueblo, Navajo, and Apache—since time immemorial have deep connections
  to the land and have made significant contributions to the broader community
  statewide. We honor the land itself and those who remain stewards of this
  land throughout the generations and also acknowledge our committed
  relationship to Indigenous peoples. We gratefully recognize our history.

Cover illustration: adapted from photograph by J. Matthew Huculak, licensed
  under CC by 4.0
Designed by Felicia Cedillos
Composed in Adobe Caslon Pro 11/14

Contents

Poems of After

For my husband—Reuven
my children—David, Allen, Ora
my grandchildren—Ariel, Ilana, Aaron, Sara, Michael.

It is with you that I eat my bread in gladness.

Foreword

ARTHUR KLEINMAN

Judith Sherman's moving volume of poetry *The Empty Bowl: Poems of the Holocaust and After* is a distillation of a life's wisdom in line with what Aristotle said was the distinguishing characteristic of such knowledge. Put simply, Aristotle held that there were three forms of knowledge: *techne*, which is a kind of technical knowledge tied to occupations and professions; *episteme*, which is knowledge about the very process of gaining knowledge; and *phronesis*, which is practical knowledge about how to live a life. Aristotle insisted it is the most important kind of knowledge. I read Judith Sherman's illuminating poems as phronesis. As she herself notes, Sherman lives on two tracks: present time and Holocaust time. That is to say, she recognizes in her experience two forms of reality, memory and attention, and of course, emotions. How do we understand what she means by this and what its more general significance represents?

To get at that issue, I believe we have to understand how the social world and the interior of our psyches connect together. Today, it is commonplace to talk about embodiment as the way the social world enters into our lived experience. But what is embodiment, and how does it connect up to poetry and aesthetic wisdom more generally? To understand that, it is worth examining the ideas of Iain McGilchrist, the British psychiatrist and humanist. In his profound meditation on the meaning for the world of our brains' right-left asymmetry, *The Master and His Emissary*, McGilchrist points out the crucial association of the propensity for writing and the appreciation of poetry with the right hemisphere's big-picture attention to the world as well as its being-in-the-world presence, its emphasis on authenticity, and its connection to musical experience and appreciation. This approach to reality stands over against the left hemisphere's propensity toward utilitarian use of language, deconstruction, and intellectualized re-presentation, which it creates along with a blindness toward what the right hemisphere brings to their necessary collaboration. For McGilchrist there is a sort of tug-of-war between these two hemispheric orientations, which usually ends up with the dominance of the left hemisphere's utilitarianism taking over because of its immediate fit with the practicalities of work and life. From this perspective, creative activities such as the writing of poetry require a liberation of the right hemisphere's orientation from the dominance of the left. This neuroscience approach seems to me one way we can understand what Judith Sherman means by living on two tracks.

The one track is our attention to the immediacy of the world, especially with respect to our need to be active in it and to wrestle with the problems and opportunities it presents to us. Most of us live our days fully absorbed with this utilitarian mode of living a life. But for those who have been deeply traumatized or who have for other reasons become unsettled by the world, there are other tracks. For example, taking a philosophical or theoretical approach to life is one such track, albeit it largely intellectual. But for creative artists like Judith Sherman, there remains the possibility of gaining immediate access to those most troubling, even terrifying, experiences of the past that exist not as representations of memory but as the actual experience itself, as it is alive in our unconscious. And in my reading of Sherman's emotion-igniting poems, that is the wisdom she creates. It is the actual experience itself emerging in words and images and presented both for its powerful illumination of pain and suffering, but also for its querying of common sense and everyday perspectives. This is the wisdom for the art of living I read in Sherman's poems about how she lived her life in Ravensbrück concentration camp . . . and after. Their powerful metaphors stop the reader in his or her tracks and force that reader to move beyond ordinary everyday reality and confront directly and without mediation the horrors of the Holocaust and the pain and suffering of the life of a survivor. Consider her poem:

Ravensbrück

The baby died—
not all at once.
at mother's breast—

baby is willing—
soon the juices stop flowing.
I walk by
and save my screams
for later.

Lord—that particular pain
is too much for me
You have it
and be
branded!

There are of course other poems in this marvelous collection that illuminate other dimensions of life from childhood to old age. She reveals a capacity for caretaking of self and others in Ravensbrück and after. For instance,

The Mirror in My Right Shoe

Here in Ravensbrück Konzentrations Lager
I see myself in a future mirror.
I find a postcard, an art reproduction of a young woman—
by Vermeer, Renoir?
Such a find is verboten. I hide her in my right shoe—
there she stays—during roll call, hunger pangs, selections;
I grow thinner, paler, weaker, shabbier, scabbier—the girl in
my shoe keeps her smirky smile, luscious tease—
her pink blouse remains clean—no green button is missing.
She is my mirror of the future—I too will grow into a young woman.
My right leg stepping into tomorrow. That girl in
my right shoe will see to it

But for me what is most crucial in the poetry is the access it gives us to what the experience of the Holocaust was like for those who lived it.

Surely this is how we will never forget. For this achievement I can only thank Sherman from the depth of my being. I shall not forget.

Preface

Telling through poems fits my telling. Life-lived themes enter the poems.

The poems in this book reflect in chronological order some of my experiences in the Holocaust, and after. I was raised in a small mountain village: Kurima, Slovakia. Terror enters my home: "a man with a bayonet is pointing at my sleeping head, happening when I am not quite ten." We are terrorized but not killed—not yet.

My death sentence is officially proclaimed when I am twelve. The Law of the Land in Slovakia (and in all places under the sphere of Nazi influence) decrees that all Jews must be "evacuated"—a euphemism for the Final Solution, the murder of all Jews. My parents are determined to defy this edict. Says my father, Ele, "All of us—some of us—one of us— must survive." Mother Ilona agrees. My chronology of this determination involves separation from family; illegal border crossings, to-and-fro; hiding in attics; Gestapo imprisonment; escape; hiding in forests; capture; wagon train; Auschwitz; imprisonment in CZ Ravensbrück; liberation. I do not die—survival is difficult—stacked against the enormity of their death-directed operation. The odds are in their favor. Note the number: 6,000,000 Jews and 5,000,000 other victims. I am a Holocaust survivor, but that past is not past. The terror of that history and the history of that terror clings.

Post-Holocaust life demands life lived on two tracks: "after" and "before." "Before" always implies the Holocaust. I do not allow the "before" to eclipse the present—but those persistent, indelible intrusions demand acknowledgment, attention. Two-track existence, accommodation— survivorship territory.

My Holocaust poems are drawn from personal history. A history that will/should always scream, "Never again." Through poems I try to make indelible memories visible and suppressed voices heard. Photographs of undeniable reality through the lens of my teenage-lived and witnessed experience. In my writing I have the urge to shrink the ugly realities into only a few words—not to soften, just to depict and hurl away. Poetry lets me do this. In addition—because during the Holocaust I have so little control of everything—the poem lets me control the structure, the boundaries, the limitations of the poem. I say what needs saying—how I want it said. My own doing.

Is it corruption to use normal words of a normal world to convey that enormous abnormality? Today certain good words have become corrupted by ugly Holocaust images: "gas," "selection," "walls." Some words will always remain loaded for me:

> <u>Bread</u>. Always, always bread. Bread is not a metaphor. Daily bread, daily had, is as good as it gets.
> <u>Survival</u>. "She built survival bricks from futile hopes."
> <u>Prayer</u>. Prisoner's morning prayer, "No more. No More. No more of that."
> <u>Loaded numbers</u>. "Prisoner 83,621 resists. Her emaciated self outnumbers the death march."
> And of course, "<u>6,000,000</u>."

In some wishful poems, I defy reality, but only in fantasy. "Stand back, you walls of ugliness."

I do not lack content for Holocaust poetry! It inhabits me.

I have an inbred inclination to believe in God and a Ravensbrück desperation to challenge God. God is a frequent theme in my poems: "are you not tempted Lord, to intervene, lend a hand, prevent a scream?" I issue God an invitation, "—then I will take Your hand and show You sites not fit for godly eyes." "Granted, Your Job directed reprimand is of good design, but what do You tell them, the Auschwitz them, shoeless and selected?"

For over fifty years, I remain almost totally silent about my Holocaust experience—silent at home, silent outside. I write poems "for my eyes only." Until Professor Davíd Carrasco of Princeton University gives ear to my silence in 2004. After his stirring lecture on the Holocaust, I identify myself as a Holocaust survivor and give him a scrap of paper with my words, "Lord, that particular pain is too much for me. You have it and be branded." He invites me to speak to his class and amazingly I agree. I seek to become witness in my writing and presentations; I give visibility to human connections in that disconnected universe, give voice to those silenced by murder. Names, I say the names: Magda, Jano, Evka—

COVID-19 has made us especially sensitive to the need for human connections. In Ravensbrück human connections are verboten, but you cannot survive without them. To share a potato, to help a fallen prisoner during *Appell* (the daily roll call), means to risk death by beating, shooting. Today, to wear a mask, to protect another from the risk of COVID death, is a minor inconvenience—yet there is resistance. Prisoners performing life-threatening small acts of kindness are the heroes of Ravensbrück. I hope to honor them in my poems. "In no other place can a friend be of such magnitude as here where a friend can do and say and be so minimally."

The enormity of the Holocaust is too enormous, but back home in Kurima what I know is too much. My soul is peopled by parents, brother, neighbors, teachers, who are no longer. Brevity is not their eulogy! Their life is. They lived, produced memories—people of life, of life, people of life.

I claim responsibility for the simple language and accessibility of my poems. The Holocaust themes and content, on the other hand, are not of my making. I am merely the witness recorder. That tale of yesterday told reluctantly, but needfully.

Liberation elicited the spirit of exodus. Expressed in, "lucky trees, we do not have to eat your leaves." Freedom from want, from all-consuming hunger, from ever-present hunger.

In my post-Holocaust life, 9/11 and genocide compel attention. I write poems about the horrors of 9/11, Darfur, Bosnia. And I write of joy and gratitude that in this splendid and unredeemed world I am gifted love, family, human connections, a garden, song. And sturdy boots, a promise I made back then, "feet, you shall have soles for your toes and options to roam in all directions." And over and over I cherish that other option, the freedom of "yes" and "no." Use has made them strut and strong.

And I too have a dream. That I in that stranger see the core of my identity—stranger see in me that core of your identity. That would address the wisdom of "your brother's keeper be." To which I would add, do add: but don't make a list of who the brother is. No list. No list. No list.

poems of before

This Time

This time
Let us be on time
Not echoes of past
Silences
Nobly moaning ignorance
This time
      On time

I Too Have a Dream

I too have a dream—
No void
No scream, no aimless feet
No hunger pangs
No armed gangs
No terror blasts into
human flesh
No cleansing of ethnicity
No leaders of duplicity
No melting of the habitat
Of penguins and of polar bears
I too have a dream—
Of daily bread
Daily had and all are fed
I too have a dream—
That I in that stranger see
The core of my identity
I too have a dream—
Stranger, see in me
The core of your identity

Because

Because of the morning sun
and Grandpa's jokes
because of the forest green
and girls who preen
because of ice cream cones
and muddy slush between my toes
because of my messy bed
and my brother's stupid head
because of all that
—I am glad

My Grandfather

A man who can peel
an apple with glee
undisturbed, unperturbed
artfully disrobing
peel from core
knows
how life
flows

Serious Men

In my small town
where the river runs deep
the red-haired miller
his two sons and son-in-law,
serious men
with serious tasks,
place sacks of
corn, rye, and barley flour
in front of other serious men
who grew the grain
and whose serious task
is done

This good season
saw grain to flour
women folk will
make the bread
—all will smell the bread
and smile,
        a serious Amen smile

poems of the Holocaust

My Village of Kurima

My village of Kurima
is in long-named Czechoslovakia.
I play in the streets—I play on the farms
where horses and buggies
outnumber the cars

I splash in the brook—in front of the house
I swim in the river—where the mill grinds the oats
My meadow grows poppies and daisies and flowers
—so blue
There isn't a color my meadow won't do!

In the back of the house
are cows—chickens and ducks
lilac and honey and milk pails and such
but you know what I wish—that I would not have to miss?
that place in the shade—of the trees with the plums
where you could rest—and make dreams—
oh—for the dreams under those trees!

And then—TERROR

A gun with a bayonet is pointing at my sleeping head
a nightmare this—but it is real
happening when
I am not quiet ten
Why is he here—this soldier—with the grin and gun
who yells at us in loud German?
"Relax you pigs—you Jewish kids
you are safe for now
the person we want—is the man with the beard
To the man with the beard
we have come to deliver a *wunderbar* treat!"

In the hall against the wall
a gun is aimed at every head
of uncles, aunts, my mom and dad
"Where is he hiding, that man with the beard
it will not go well if you do not tell!"
they finally leave—they finally go
now all of us know—the taste and the feel
of TERROR and FEAR

Though Hitler resides in Germany
his rules apply to my country:
"Jews—you wear a yellow star,
stay indoors when it is dark,
give up your fields—lock up your stores
don't sit in parks—don't mingle with the Aryans!"

Grandma is sad—she has lost the rights
to her candlesticks—for Shabbat lights
then Grandma says, "God do not fret,
I will make a light that's brighter yet!"
She lights the candles on a stone
and adds to this her special glow

It Is the Law

It is the law
it is the law
out of my hands
it is the law

How, in all those
hymnal holding
hands—
impotence?

The Law of the Land

No! This Law of the Land
will not be the end
of Judit and Karpu not Miru so small
not Mother—not me—to hell with your *Heil*
We will defy—we will survive
All of us—some of us
One of us—
Together—in pairs—most likely alone
We will hide in some attic
cross borders by night
seek shelters in ditches
sleep in the forest—crouch under bridges
When this Law of the Land
comes to an end
All of us—some of us
maybe just one of us
maybe just one of us
will defy—will survive

My Suitcase and I

Ruthie says I do not understand
why Mama and Papa and Rudy, my dog
stay outside while inside the train
my suitcase and I sit silent and scared

The Germans are here—says Papa to me—
You must go to England on Kindertransport.
I am six and do not know why Germans
are bad and England is safe.

My suitcase and I, my suitcase and I
my mama does say with tears in her eyes—
You will find what you need in this suitcase from home.
In this suitcase from home I find a photograph
of Papa and Mama smiling for me.

The letters to England come many at first
then lesser and fewer
then none come at all.

Today I am a woman of generous years.
my suitcase is worn, its markings are many
the photo inside is faded and gray
but a memory-maker day by day.

My suitcase, my suitcase, my suitcase and I,
are grateful to England for keeping us safe
but sad that England did not
make a Grownup transport

My suitcase, my suitcase, my suitcase and I . . .

Morning Mass

At 5 a.m.
roaming this city
of bolted doors
I hear my intensified heart
outsound the church bells
inviting the faithful
to 6 a.m. mass
come all ye faithful
glorify Him—Christ the son
[the Jewish son]

At 6 a.m. will bolted
doors unlock for me?
At 6 a.m. where will I be?
will I be?

Toothbrush

Imprisoned in Hungary
I cry—how can I not cry
When I do not have a toothbrush?!
A person without a toothbrush
Is a person without—
Toothbrush starts your day
Ends your day—
A grounding ritual.
Later in KZ Ravensbrück
Toothbrush is not a necessity
Feel of toothbrush
Taste of peppermint toothpaste—
Luxury from another world.
In Ravensbrück no luxuries
No necessities either.
I no longer cry.

Gestapo Prison

I recognize you who passed through
and left your marks
on these prison walls

your years a tale
of harmonica sounds
of planted corn
mended shoes

you carried little ones across the brook
you prayed—you whistled
fixed the roofs and lit the lamps
made bread—made wine
danced and teased
drank buttermilk

fear not, fear not
may these walls rot
ere I forget
your years, your tales,
your brevity

you who come here
after me recount
my tale, my years,
my brevity

Mirjam's Letter from Hiding

Why does that woman brush my hair
and make my braids so tight?
That brush is wrong!
I need my purple one
from home.

Here—I should not be,
my second grade is missing me.

I like the dog—
him I told
my birthday came
and no one called.

All my life—and all the time
I have this name that's really mine
now, hear this—Mirjam-it-is!
Mirjam, Mirjam, Mirjam—is me!
but she says "child, Maria, it must be."

They say I cannot go outside to play
I may forget who I am not—
it is not wise—too great a risk
for a Jewish child to play outside
That—I do not understand
I do not want to understand!
I want to go outside and play
but here I must what others say)

I hate that here I cannot do
what at home I hate to do:
walk the dog—get up for school,
wear dresses, hats to services

The mail in your vicinity
was stopped by some authority
no matter—I have a plan that is much better.
(and besides—
I have no paper on which to write.)
I will send this letter from my brain
and you will get it right away:

come and get me—I am ready
bring my doll—the orange ribbons
cookies in a special box
I would like that quite a lot.

P.S. I will have to hide
when you ring the bell
but I will know you
I will know you by your smell.

Unhiding in the Forest

When war is done
I will metamorphosize
into visibility
I'll wear scarlet
I'll make noises,
invite echoes

Bonfires and picnic baskets
I'll bring along a friend
or two or three or seventy

I'll leave the berries
to the birds
I will not fear
your din of thrush or brush
nor fear
lest a human should appear

Trees dense or sparse,
what's it to me?
I'll be cloaked into visibility!
Hang in there
wait for me
and I will do my best
to be

Hiding in the Forest

We hide in the forest—me and few others.
Does it make sense—to be wet and cold
With so much wood all around?
The potatoes we eat are always raw
Eggs and milk I never saw.
NO FIRE—NO FIRE—by night or day
A fire in this place would give you away!
The berries we pick are good as a treat
But meal after meal—and day after day
My teeth protest—"No More—No More
No More of that!"
I do not complain, no one does
Would that be of use to us?

We plan and we guess which way to go
Due south or due north—later or now?
Do we stay with the groups—or split up in twos?
The wrong answer—means disaster.
So out in that forest—under that sky
There isn't a route that we do not try

"Get up! Mach schnell—you dirty Jews!"
The soldiers appear—with dogs and guns
Those of us who try to run—are chased and shot
The chase is pleasing to the dogs.
We are marched to the trucks—we travel light
All we have we leave behind.

In prison now—the dogs are fed
The dogs did fine—the forest now is Judenrein.

"Give us your gold, your rings, your cash
You greedy Jews have much of that!"
(In my own mind I am confused
—is it not they who take from us
And take and grab and look for more
And get real mad—when nothing more is to be had?)

Karpu in Auschwitz

eight—perhaps as much as nine
I teased him around our kitchen table.
Did anyone want to, care to,
was strong enough to
touch his pale hair
when gas was filling?
and his breathing
his breathing
I want to be there
and help him breathe
and postpone dying
and I do not want
to die
until he does
and—and—

(Karpu, my brother, will forever be nine)

Such Good Taste

I overheard
Hauptmann Kurt
say to
Kapitan Schmidt
"Leisel will like
this gold watch.
She has such
good taste.
Die Judin
wanted water in
return.
Stupid swine,
always water.
Always asking."

Wagon Train

too high
too small
too barred
too walled
this window of the wagon train
no air
no room
no space
for rage

look in, Lord
and record
indelibly—
stone tablets
break easily

I am your God
your only God
in My image
created I you.

where My image?
I seek My image

Lord what of those
who bolt these doors
seek You there
Your Holy sphere?

Your image?

Auschwitz

du hast glick
du furst a weg
alles is besser wie Auschwitz
whispers the man in stripes
pushing me back into the wagon train—
my *glick*—my luck—
no room in the gas chamber
ten thousand Hungarian Jews gassed this hour
in KZ Ravensbrück
our new destination
selections and gassing operate
I survive Auschwitz
Auschwitz—my *glick*

Lord

Are you not tempted—Lord
to intervene
to lend a hand
prevent a scream?

SS Man

Do you have nightmares?
your polished boots
under your bed, blood stained
Do you say "obedience is the law,
loyalty is the law,
über alles"?
Do you tell your children
of the children
who stained your boots?
Do you have nightmares?

Knew You Then

Before you knew
what now you do, before that
did you pat a cat?
wear summer shoes
before those boots?
bow before the Holy cross
ere you hailed the Haken Kreuz?
and did you throw a ball
tease a girl
practice how
to tie a tie
and help your grandad
unknot the net?

that, before you crushed
the skull
of a sweet-haired child?

knew you then
the ways of men?
the ways of men
stead of the bloated supermen?

be damned if you forgot
be double damned
if you did not

Morning Prayer

Shriek—you day ahead
Shriek: no more—
no more—no more—
no more of that!

During *Appell*

When she fell
during *Appell*
the women around her
being new
bent down toward her
—automated responses still—
they never straightened up
could not
after shots and dogs
—this did not affect
the body count

Appell Guard

After morning *Appell*
she crosses the camp gate
greets a friend
has leftover bread for breakfast
writes a letter
MENSCHLICHKEIT
Evening *Appell*—beats prisoners

Magda Speaks Kein Deutsch

Magda speaks Kein Deutsch
Kein Deutsch is not good
in this land of supermen.
"Magda," I say, "do what I do—line up for work
for soup—selections—delousing."
Magda into my shadow grows
—thinness amplified.
"My friend," she says, "here is my
bread
a gift for you for all you do."

A gift of bread—a gift of life
and more than that
a rest from hunger
that will not rest.

Two days later Magda lies
dead,
I am relieved I made her keep
that gift of bread.

(Oh. I do not lack for
choiceless remembrances.)

I do not shorten Magda's life,
but I wish that I could have
a moment
full—of—bread

Come, Messiah

Come, Messiah
when blossoms quiver
the cow is milked
children bathed
and done with measles.
The week's Torah
portion read
and fathers rest

If this is not
convenient
come then in times
of empty udders,
typhoid, lice, and lamentations,
prayers said—not read
(the Written Word
in flames of amber was
returned to the Sender)
It would suit us fine
if you made this
Messiah time

Is not the Apocalypse
your cue
to do
the Messiah
thing?

Hunger

First I make sure
I have my bowl and my spoon
then
with empty bowl
and spoon in hand,
I practice eating, lest
—I forget
lest I forget

Hunger, Do Not Intrude

Hunger, do not intrude
do not chagrin
do not shrill
do not presume
you are my all
you, you are
not my all
at all!

Now note you this:
—my Genesis!

Sun, be warm
be warm, Sun
hunger does not
let you in
I am always shivering

Crocuses be purple-pink
bees do not sting!
matching buttons
for my coat. Scratch that!
A new coat
pale pale gray, a
new comb for my
new hair

No barren soup
no turnips
no black water

A big book
hardcovered
visible

Sing birds
green songs, loud, louder
than their rifle shots
Gooseberry jam,
friends, cousins
(a boy in sandals
watches me
me, a hit? so be it)

Neighbor lady
look at me
God Almighty
dance with me

Let Not Flowers Here

Let not flowers here
        not scented rose
        not meadow hues
        not daffodils
        not silver dew

a bird in flight
would fry
on voltaged walls
higher than the sky

no Edenic scenes for me
Edenic scenes a mockery!
crushed and crazed
indignant

I would be
when tortured
amid
splendidly

The Invitation

Would You come down
that ladder—that ladder
Jacob climbed?
I will not deal with angels, I will
wait till You arrive

When You come down That
ladder—that ladder
Jacob climbed
then I will take Your hand
and I will be Your
guide and You
will see sights
not fit for
Godly eyes

Not fit for Thee
—is it for me?

For Your divine grief
I would hand a handkerchief
have none
nor am I in need of one
we save our tears
water shortage

An Apple in Ravensbrück

I once saw
an apple
in Ravensbrück.
The apple-eater
with boots and whip
and warm warm coat
—but we the hungry
saw the apple only.
And You, Lord
what did You see?
Do You no longer
kick apple-eaters
out of Paradise?
her Ravensbrück Paradise?
Explain, please

My Ravensbrück Love Song

One Sunday
that April
the Sun came by
I untangled my hair

With the hem of my dress
wiped the mud off my shoes
then—in proper attire
I set forth

Not today
you stupid walls of ugliness!
today
I decree
plum trees. Crickets, and green things
for me

On the street with a name
—no numbers today
we meet—Yano and me
I am early
as is he.
His mother liked me
"that blue-eyed girl"
would she be pleased,
her Yano and me?

Stand back you stupid walls
stand back!
Today we will not be
walled in—
Not Yano
not me

P.S. Yano died in Auschwitz gas chamber.
I defy reality, but only in fantasy.

I Know a Dog

I know a dog
I named him Ben
I named him Ben
when I was ten.
Oh—I could tell a lot
about that dog—But take my word
when you encounter him
you—grin—and—grin.

I know a dog
his name is Hund
his master with the
whip and gun only
lets this big dog run to kill
and maim
and snare and bite
those of us
who are still alive

I do not know
if Hund is pleased
to live a life of kill
or leash.
(they taught him well
—he does not falter
this brute extension
of his master)
to encounter him
is—grim—so—grim.

choose
your friend
Hund or Ben

Ravensbrück

The baby died—
not all at once.
at mother's breast
baby is willing—
soon the juices stop flowing.
I walk by
and save my screams
for later.

Lord—that particular pain
is too much for me
You have it
and be
branded!

Jesus, Tell Your Father

Tell your Father
who art in Heaven
His will be done
and you want
Ephraim's good name cleared
Loud and cleared.

Granted I have no claim
on you
but being of the same
family
a name
tarnished
harms
It is time—
tell Him

Stand Still, Sun

Stand still, Sun
make dark the world

spotlight this site
of primal night

where women shrink
rats bloat

let the wise men come
let the wise men see

mother and child
mother no child

orphaned child
no mother no child

this inn does all accommodate
as ashen skies regurgitate

The Roma Girl

The Roma girl
has one shoe,
the left shoe

Inside the shoe
an orange rag
right up to her knee,
formerly her right-hand
sleeve

Mutter? she asks of every
woman
in her path.
A hundred, thousand, million
Mutter? Mutter? Mutter?

That Roma child
never gets it
right

Ravensbrück Friend

In no other
place can a
friend
say and do
and be
a friend
of
such magnitude
as here
where a friend
can say
and
do and be
so minimally

Shoes for Life

I shall never not value shoes,
life is from the ground up.
Life with shoes—
perhaps
without—death

They know the value of shoes.
do they not keep the shoes
and dispose of the wearer?
no discrimination
—all sizes valued

The Mirror in My Right Shoe

Here in Ravensbrück Konzentrations Lager
I see myself in a future mirror.
I find a postcard, an art reproduction of a young woman—
by Vermeer, Renoir?
Such a find is verboten. I hide her in my right shoe—
there she stays—during roll call, hunger pangs, selections;
I grow thinner, paler, weaker, shabbier, scabbier—the girl in
my shoe keeps her smirky smile, luscious tease—
her pink blouse remains clean—no green button is missing.
She is my mirror of the future—I too will grow into a young woman.
My right leg stepping into tomorrow. That girl in
my right shoe will see to it

A Brief Reprieve

I do not wish to forget,
just a brief reprieve
to remember
seasonal shoes
open-toed or snow-
resistant; a lunch table
with rolls
left over;
a muscled father in
charge—humorously
comforting a
a scraped knee;
a whim, a laughing dog
Shabbath candles
gray hair

I wish to remember
the place "before"
before the "after"
overlay

Before—for a while
before I die

You Are Invited to My Funeral

You are invited
to my funeral
to my un-Auschwitz funeral.
Attire of choice—
no stripes please.
Come nearer,
come nearer
and attest
that beneath this poplar tree,
this season-marking poplar tree
in this pleasant ground
chosen and paid for—
with space reserved nearby
for husband to join
in timely manner
for company and closeness—
attest people,
that Yehudit
the person Yehudit
Yehudit the Jew
is according to custom
here buried.
You come too, Lord.
(were You too embarrassed to
attend in Auschwitz?)
You come too, Lord
and smile—
Your will be done.
No! Not smile!
Just be

Reluctant Witness

Am I to be that mariner
And retell that tale of yesteryear?
I am not him!
I did not sin!
—

Hereby I testify
To THEIR murder of:
Anna—death by starving
Evka—death by beating
Daniel—death by gassing
Lily—by hanging
Ivan—typhoid
Peter—drowning
Johana—starving and shooting
Mrs. Rheinhardt—by choice—to avoid the above
Chayim—death by living

Where is the Judge?
Where are you, Judge?
Is there a Judge?

Resistance of Prisoner 83,621

Prisoner 83,621 resists:
she hides in the attic, she sleeps in the forest
in Camp she washes daily under the waterless tap;
she does not steal her bunkmate's bread,
shares the stolen potato
resists suicidal death relief at electric fence;
utters verboten prayers, thinks verboten thoughts
of home, of hair, of greening soil—
and names, and names, the sound of names;
she makes secret friends in a friendless world,
erects survival bricks from futile hopes,
kills fatted lice, dreads the dogs, envies warm SS coats;
she emits no overt cry, complaint, or rage—futile this and forbidden,
saves her nonexistent strength to survive today's selection—
one day's survival measures Camp's eternity;
she spoons the empty soup bowl to practice eating
—lest she forget;
at times she sings Mother's songs—but not the German ones,
she sends unwritten letters to President Roosevelt,
sends reminder invitations to God and Messiah;
defies the plan—her emaciated self outmarches,
outmarches the Death March;

Prisoner 83,621 resists and lives—
around me, nameless, numbered, prisoners resist and die.
Let no one say—"They went to death like sheep"
DARE NO ONE SAY THEY WENT TO DEATH LIKE SHEEP

Death March

When unshod
a faster gait
prevents the feet
from sticking to
the ice and sleet

when shod in clogs
bruised and sore
a slower pace
is preferred

The commandant
and his crew
through
planned precision knew
that either step
would do
to undo

I Say Damn You

I say damn you
I say a corpse
I say a shooting
I say a dog
let loose,
I say damn you
I say damn you
be damned I say
because I say
a corpse a shooting
a dog let loose
with ease

Liberation

Liberation is women washing potatoes by the pump

Preparing our first meal of freedom

Liberation is sitting on a chair

Liberation is messing around with the door, open—close—open

Drinking from a cup

Hearing birds

Trees, I Say

The trees are
growing leaves,
I say, Lucky trees
we do not have to
eat your leaves

Cat, I say
do not strut,
like you, I too can
come and go
without
accountability

God, I say,
I will
not sacrifice,
but come and
share
our fresh baked bread

Death, Stand Aside at My Liberation Time

Death, stand aside
do not hover by
my side!
Watch, I leap
touch the sun
stop motor cars
wear sandals that
are open-toed

I run, I hum
am everywhere.
Don't mess with me
you bloated creep
you cannot
run as fast
as me!

poems of after

Once You Survive

Once you survive,
a sated body and no lice
do not suffice—
I am glad of that
in there I thought
such state to be
the kindest fate

No More Hide-and-Seek

Paulie and I played hide-and-seek
he hides I seek—I hide he seeks;
but now I alone hide hide hide—
and they with boots, dogs, and guns
seek, seek, and seek;
when war is done I want to be
nine, and ten, and thirty-three;
when war is done I will have
hot chocolate and bread
with Grandma's raspberry jam;
I will have many birthdays and grow a
mustache like my papa and a gray beard
like my grandpapa—they too were seeked and they were found
—I have their photographs to guide me;
after the war I will open all the windows
in the world,
I will have a dog for play and name him Lee
short for Paulie
now hear this—after the war I will make a law
I will shout out loud—
no HIDE and SEEK allowed—any place any time—
never any more—HIDE and SEEK!
never HIDE and SEEK any more

Tell Me This

Tell me, tell me, tell me this
I must know, for I am six

Grass is green—white is the snow
please tell me why this is so?

I can hear the night escaping
but where is tomorrow waiting?

who scares the lion—that mighty beast
is it the sting of the bumblebee?

who wetted the ocean—who salted the sea
who made my leg bend right at the knee?

when rain puddles mess up my toes
why does my heart sing out so loud?

tell me questions not asked yet—
do all questions have an answer?

This Year in Jerusalem

This year in Jerusalem
on the shores of Ashkelon
with might of tides
with roar of sea
and stiller than the olive tree
and louder than the desert wind
and sweeter than the
Song of Songs
            —more ardent than
the shofar blast
as honest as
an infant's smile
as hope-filled
as a field of wheat
            —I shall pray for Peace

That You Should Know

That you should know
you, blessed by God
and well-shod fathers,
should know

of shoeless fathers
ashen boys
sated dogs and
shorn women

know of
polluting skies
blinding the angels
and hiding
God

Legacy Poem

Bread, always bread
stars that lighten the heavens
not brand your chests
always, always—water
trains to journeys of delight
with seats, windows,
tickets of return
no accent
fathers to hold your children's hand
children who outgrow their shoes
your mantle of "Jew"
of cloth so light
so safe
so Kol B'Seder
mothers—oh yes—mothers—
mothers you can stand up to!
Israel to fill your soul

And what of Auschwitz memory?
That too is in your legacy

Do Something

Enough bathtub
meditations
synchronize
the oceans!

Accountability

Accountability
is Divinity

9/11: Has Anybody Seen My Dad?

Has anybody seen my dad?
His name is Arnie—
Arnie . . . is my dad
He wears a tie
that's purple-pink
the one that I
have given him

Oh, you'd recognize my dad,
between his front teeth
there is a gap,
probably the reason why
on this photograph
he does not smile

Did you see my dad?
My dad called home on the cell phone,
told my mom
"there is a fire
and I cannot see—
I love you, Ellie
and tell the kids
I . . ."

Have you seen my dad?
The hospitals say
"No, not yet,
not yet, not yet"

You call if you see my dad,
and I'll keep looking for you, Dad
Please God, oh, God
where is my dad?
Where—is—my—dad?
—

Her life will go on, and she will keep looking

My Darfur Mother

My mother sits
upon bareness,
watching, unseeing
watching,
her wounded memory
of shrieking cows
slain husband
drowned son

I, her ripped daughter,
curse you, you prayer-
mouthing, you freedom-
spouting
you ALWAYS AGAIN
standbys
Be you cursed with
my mother's memory

Bosnia Boy

She is no longer
I put the flowers for my teacher
on her funeral box

no more school
I know enough

I must not sleep
they shoot they hit
they push make pain
and when I sleep
they come again

nine-year-old boy
father holds me
on his
lap
holds me, holds me
holds me—don't move, no sound
like that

my friend Andrei
buried in his old clothes—
his new white shirt new trousers
new cap, socks—for school
useless

his mother lives
how will she?
both sons missing

To Walk in My Shoes

To walk in my shoes
you must feel in your toes
you must know in your heart
that like you—folks the world over
need bread in the morning
and comfort at night.
You must know—you must know
that people all over need shelter
and safety, and laughter and song.
Come, stranger, walk in my shoes
and cherish your own—
and step by step and hand in hand
let us connect the universe

I Smile, I Smile

The garden I garden
Seduces the soul
Mocking all shortcuts
Demands honest toil
That geranium there
Dares
Such rightness
Such red!

At crocus times
I smile
I smile

The garden I garden
Knows
When—what color—
How

And I know this
For soul to taste the soil
For bliss like this
You must a touch of Genesis

Fresh Washed Sheets

I am in love with
fresh washed sheets
my flowerbeds
the coffee shop
at every stop;
I love the zest of my love's quest
the spunk of grandchild
when sent to bed;
the pink stone of Jerusalem
the pleasing sound
Je-ru-sa-lem;
my hair when wet
from morning rain
a friend who says
let's lunch again;
a daughter's new maturity
in styling herself after me;
I am in love with
"enough for now"
I am in love with
"I want more"
I am in love with
fresh washed sheets
and purple-red anemones

Sunrise

Copper-purple clad
you wake the world

making the corn
heighten,
the ice shrink

at morn, human hearts
read possibility in
your undiminished potency;
at morn—hope

(as for
me—I would so
like a clue
who birthed the birther
who birthed you?)

Summer Woods

In this millennium year
I would like to see a summer wood
I would like to see a summer wood and
not worry
Is it deep enough—dense enough
to hide me?

In this millennium year
I say
it is now far enough—late enough
to live here now—
        so let the shower be just that
        and the railway tracks—
        potatoes too—see they are plentiful
but how do you disconnect
from KZ Ravensbrück?

I am old in this year of two thousand
but my soul—my soul
is peopled with parents
who are younger than my children
My brother will forever be nine.

I wish for a cemetery with gravestones
with the name of—with the name of—
with the name of—
Lord, it would help
if You would light some candles
say Kaddish—
they would appreciate that
me too
You too—perhaps?

In this millennium year
I will also plant a garden
visit Barcelona and Jerusalem
swim with grandchildren.
survivorship territory—
multiple residences
lived in simultaneously—
this place / that other place.

World, I have a question in this millennium year—
two thousand years of ethnic cleansing—
who is clean?

In this millennium year
I wish for us to see
the Summer Woods.

If God Is Dead

If God is dead
where is He dead
above which Auschwitz sky?
At rest perhaps in garden's shade
in empty Eden's grace?
Where do we light the candle
if God is dead?
If God is dead
we must not leave Him
unattended—
nor us
        nor us

Are Things Changed in Heaven?

Granted. Your Job directed
reprimand is well crafted
and of high design,

and what do You tell them,
the Auschwitz them,
when last seen
shoeless and selected?

What say You to the killers
and those who know not
know not?

By what name do we call You?
(oh, make this nonnegotiable)
are things changed in heaven
as they are on earth?

When You come down
that ladder—that ladder
Jacob climbed,
I will hold on tight
for answers
and for You

How You Are?

Lord, I would so like to know
how You are—Your noontime stroll,
the company You keep,
those angels, does
their perfection bore You—irritate?
those flapping wings
—I prefer the sound of feet,
they jealous
of us in Your likeness made,
resent our recalcitrance?
Lord, You been—done all
need a challenge?
Teach me to speak without
an accent

Oversight

Lord, had You given
us
Eden—and
awareness, You
could have moved
in
with us.

If You Apologize

God, I would—
tentatively—enter
Your Game Plan,
if You apologize
for my hesitations.

Let Me Win

I have touched the bottom rung
of love's approximation,
higher I dared not

When I myself have blessed
I will take on
the angel

Impartial God
let me
win.

A Ladder for God

I shall pile
the pleas from
the Wailing Wall
stack helmets of
the fallen
into a ladder
for God
to descend
and make peace
on Earth

We Should Talk

We should talk.
This half century later
we should talk—
two grandmothers we should talk.
I cannot bear
to wear
stripes

Your swastika
safely sheltered in
family Bible
tissue wrapped, is it?
Your glory days

That blue-gray coat
high polished boots
seen by downcast
untermensch eyes
(blue like yours)
I remember

Your glory days
Your dog so helpful
so obedient
so well trained
(they don't make them like that anymore)

Me a blur—or—less in your eyes
that messy field of thousand thousand
blurs—that vision cleared.
—Judenrein

Is to-day to-day for you?
Is there doubt,
hesitation?
Glory days
We should talk
Should we talk?

Survivor's Voice Today

Today we have age lines
and laugh lines
and sturdy shoes—a promise we kept
when way way back we said
"feet, we you shall have soles for your toes
and splendid options to roam
in all directions"

Today we say—yes, we say—no
feel our muscled choices
use has made them strut and strong

Today we know this—
daily bread—daily had is
as good as it gets

And we know too
a body is a mighty awe
a body is a tale of all
World, to save your soul
let the body be

Today we know love
today we know song
our children are grand
our grandchildren grander

And today and day after day
for seventy years
we are owned by a past we cannot abandon
in our souls in our pores
we are where they are and bring them along
and take them along
in acts of day in dreams of night

Today we are old, our tale is told
you witness to witness
be garbed in care
be girded by strength
and see to it—see to it
that our tale does not repeat

Survivor's Message

to witness I say: your tale that should not be must be told
to every child in village and town

to teachers I declare: math, science, and literacy compute into
monstrosity if not anchored in humanity

at all—I rage, I rage: ethnic cleansing—who is clean?!
what way clean?! clean of what?!—discard, uproot, eliminate this
Uber Alles—legacy

World—I say: your brother's keeper be
but don't make a list—no list—no list—of who the brother is

people, I say: as water fills the sea,
let our works our deeds
produce a mighty stream

Say the Name

Say the name
Announce, pronounce
Recite the name
Six million times the name, the name

You master race
Who smashed and gassed
—erased the name,
You callous world disdained
their fate,
I order you to
Script, engrave,
Imprint the name
And say and say and say the name,
When every name is said and heard
Repeat the name again again

May you outlive eternity
And say the name eternally
<#>
God, please attend
God, please assure
That every name
Is accounted for

Afterword

ILANA GELB

My grandmother began to enact her resistance during the Holocaust for a public audience in her first book, *Say the Name: A Survivor's Tale in Prose and Poetry*. She told of her early childhood, her family's efforts to evade the Nazis, her imprisonment in Ravensbrück concentration camp, and, finally, her liberation. After fifty years of public silence, my grandmother wrote loudly, bravely, and beautifully about her survival of the Holocaust. Following the book's publication, invitations to provide Holocaust education poured in. She gave many presentations to audiences as diverse as rural middle schools, regional Holocaust education centers, Princeton University, and the Harvard University Divinity School.

She remains resolute that her tale will be heard, lest history continue to repeat itself.

> Today we are old, our tale is told
> you witness to witness
> be garbed in care
> be girded by strength
> and see to it—see to it
> that our tale does not repeat.

After two decades of sharing her story publicly, she embarked upon her second book, *The Empty Bowl: Poems of the Holocaust and After*. The Nazis sentenced my grandmother to death at age twelve. To publish a book of poetry in her older years is resistance. In *The Empty Bowl*, she creates art, builds legacy, brings voice to the voiceless. She defies Nazi orders.

In "Poems of the Holocaust," my grandmother shares her tale of resistance and survival before and during the war. She begins at home in her village of Kurima, Czechoslovakia, declaring her family's protest of the Nazi regime. At first by defying new anti-Semitic laws and policies, by burying the shabbat candlesticks, by hiding in the forest, then by sustaining the determination to live.

> All of us—some of us
> maybe just one of us
> maybe just one of us
> will defy—will survive

In Ravensbrück concentration camp, my grandmother resisted through maintaining ritual, building friendships, practicing her humanity. She feels anger, sings songs, picks lice, debates with God. She describes her getting out of bed to the sound of *Appell*, rollcall, each morning in the camp as "resistance—a gift to her family and friends." The alternative would be death.

> Prisoner 83,621 resists:
> she hides in the attic, she sleeps in the forest
> in Camp she washes daily under the waterless tap;
> she does not steal her bunkmate's bread,
> shares the stolen potato.

This book is a testament to my grandmother's willful resistance to dehumanization in the face of unimaginable pain and violence.

In "Poems of After," she reflects with the reader on her life after the war.

> Once you survive
> A sated body and no lice
> Do not suffice—
> I am glad of that
> In there I thought
> Such state to be
> The kindest fate

My grandma is determined not only to survive, but to exude life. In her writing it is clear that she is an orator of wit, grower of gardens, consumer of literature. She is a leader in her community, matriarch of children and grandchildren, convener of poetry groups, advocate of social justice.

My grandmother's poems reveal to us her ongoing quest to explore her questions about God, accountability, identity, and legacy. From an unpublished essay:

> Those years ago I do not die—
> Though my death sentence is proclaimed
> Years revolving into life's flow
> Family garden, gray hair

Since her death sentence was proclaimed, my grandmother's very existence is resistance. My grandma keeps her hair short—a defiance after the Nazis did not have time to shave her head in the camp. She does not examine fruit at the supermarket—a dissent to selections in Ravensbrück. She is fiercely proud of her Jewish identity—and openly wrangles with God. On fasting holidays, she has a large breakfast in protest of God. She already starved in Ravensbrück. And then she fasts the rest of the day in homage to her faith in Judaism and her Kurima family.

> Today we say—yes; we say—no;
> feel our muscled choices
> use has made them strut and strong

Her ability to make choices is resistance, her exercise of these choices further so. In her poetry, readers will discover my grandmother's process of deciding how to survive: what it means to her to be a survivor, to bear a survivor's voice, and to enact a survivor's legacy. Through her writing, she not only shares her story, but also accountability and demands.

> That tale inhabits me
> World, make room for my tale
> I am not space enough

Her Holocaust story must be shared. And it is only one part of her legacy. Readers will also encounter Judith Sherman as a friend, scholar, mother, grandmother, rebel, artist, philosopher, debater, comedian, theologian, and activist.

My grandma is steadfast in her commitment to spread the practice of *tikkun olam*—"world repair"—a theme that emanates clearly throughout her poetry. She asks of us readers to recount her tale and to implement her message in our daily lives:

> This time
> Let us be on time
> Not echoes of past
> Silences
> Nobly moaning ignorance
> This time"
>   On time

With this book, she amplifies the messages of those who did not survive. She defies Nazi orders through her quest to live loudly and fully. And she shares with us the responsibility to carry on this legacy.

Acknowledgments

The content of my poems is the expression of my Holocaust experience and life after. Putting this indelible content into words parallels the development of a photograph from the negative into a visible image. Of course, this process predates the technology of the "smartphone." Historically, for over half a century these poems were written "for my eyes only." I am grateful that the University of New Mexico Press is now publishing this collection and giving it visibility. I am grateful.

I thank Professor Davíd Carrasco for reconnecting me with the Press as he did initially for my book *Say the Name*. He has consistently encouraged and urged my voice into witnessing. Michael Millman, my editor at the Press, showed an immediate interest in my poems and caringly fostered and shepherded the process leading to publication. I am grateful for his interest, guidance, and availability throughout.

I thank Jehanne Dubrow and Hilda Raz for their very helpful suggestions regarding the structure and organization of the manuscript. I implemented these changes, and this made my writing more effective. Of course, I am most appreciative of their very positive evaluation of the poems themselves.

Sara—you did the scanning and the planning, and you always put my best foot forward.

Ilana—a granddaughter for the ages.

Son David—without your tech skills and organizational assistance, my book of poems would have remained a longhand manuscript forever. You helped and helped and helped some more. Thank you.

A Holocaust survivor lives on two tracks always—here and there—now and before. My family—you anchor me into the life of love and normalcy. You make the difference.

Contributors

Judith Sherman was born in Czechoslovakia. She is a Holocaust survivor of the Ravensbrück concentration camp, Germany. She is the author of *Say the Name: A Survivor's Tale in Prose and Poetry* and has presented widely on the Holocaust. She is a graduate of the London School of Economics and Political Science and holds master's degrees in counseling and social work from Queens College and Adelphi University. She has also completed a number of postgraduate fellowships in marriage and family therapy and has worked as a therapist and clinical supervisor.

Arthur Kleinman is the Rabb Professor of Anthropology at Harvard and a professor of global health and social medicine and of psychiatry at Harvard Medical School. He is the author of *The Illness Narratives*, *What Really Matters*, and *The Soul of Care* and is a member of the National Academy of Medicine and the American Academy of Arts and Sciences.

Ilana Gelb, Judith Sherman's granddaughter, was born in New York. She joined Sherman in multigenerational Holocaust presentations from the age of thirteen to the present. Like her grandmother, she graduated from the London School of Economics and Political Science with a master of science in international development and humanitarian emergencies and obtained a bachelor of arts from the City University of New York in violence, conflict, and human rights. After working in humanitarian contexts across four continents, Gelb currently works in humanitarian affairs and global health policy in New York.